# LIFE IS SHORT

### EIGHT SHORT COMEDIES
### BY CRAIG POSPISIL

★

★

DRAMATISTS
PLAY SERVICE
INC.

LIFE IS SHORT
Copyright © 2005, Craig Pospisil

All Rights Reserved

*for my grandmother,*
*Lucile Distad,*
*who's life has been long and full*

*and in memory of my grandparents,*
*Arnold Distad*
*&*
*Albina and Charles Pospisil*

# AUTHOR'S NOTE

*Life is Short* came into being as an offshoot of another play. Three of the scenes in this collection — "Class Conflict," "Double Wedding" and "The Last December" — were originally part of my play *Months on End*. The idea behind *Months* was to write a short play for and inspired by each month of the year, and these were the original "September," "June" and "December" scenes, respectively. As *Months* evolved, the play became more realistic and these scenes no longer worked with the direction the play as a whole had moved, and, sadly, had to be removed.

Looking at the three scenes, however, I noticed an arc going from childhood to marriage to old age. I began to imagine a new collection of short works, focusing on the kind of changes and challenges that each decade of life brings. As I worked on new short plays for various festivals and showcases, I wrote some with an eye to fitting them into this arc of a life span. So now, a few years later, *Life is Short* completes a cycle that began with *Months on End*. These plays are different in style and content, but they can be done together as a single evening of theater or separately.

I'd like to thank a number of people who helped me during the evolution of the pieces that make up *Life is Short*: Jay Zimmerman; the members of the Workshop at the Neighborhood Playhouse — particularly Harold Baldridge, Darcie Siciliano, Michael Locascio, & Jim Brill; Stage Shadows Productions ("Radio like you've never seen it!"); Patricia Watt and the Manhattan Drama Collective; the Metropolitan Playhouse — particularly Alex Roe and Tony Pennino; Tom Rowan; Patricia McLaughlin; the members of Playwrights Actors Contemporary Theater and most especially the lovely and inspiring Katherine Jane Petrov.

# CONTENTS

# CLASS CONFLICT

CLASS CONFLICT was originally produced under the title "September" by the Workshop at the Neighborhood Playhouse (Harold Baldridge, Artistic Director) as part of *Months on End*, on May 24, 1998. It was directed by Tom Dybek, and the cast was as follows:

BILLY ................................................................. Andrew Donovan
MEGAN DEVENAUX ................................................ Jane Jepson

## CHARACTERS

BILLY — 6, but to be played by an adult
MEGAN DEVENAUX — 6, also to be played by an adult

## PLACE

A classroom.

## TIME

The first day of school.

# CLASS CONFLICT

*A classroom, with small, child-sized seats. Billy, age six (but played by an adult) sits in one of the chairs, waiting. A moment later Megan, also six (also played by an adult), enters. Billy is dressed casually like a six-year-old might dress, but Megan is dressed more like a tiny lawyer. She carries a lunch box that looks like a leather briefcase. Megan takes in the room, nose in the air. Billy watches her.*

BILLY.  Hi.

MEGAN.  How do you do.

BILLY.  *(Slight pause.)* What?

MEGAN.  I said, "How do you do?"

BILLY.  Oh. *(Pause.)* My name's Billy.

MEGAN.  I am Megan Devenaux.

BILLY.  Oh. *(Pause.)* Are you scared? I'm a little scared. I wish my mommy was here. She told me the first day of school was nothing to be afraid of. But I am.

MEGAN.  Never let them see your fear.

BILLY.  Oh. *(Pause.)* What?

MEGAN.  Always project a bold, fuck-you attitude.

BILLY.  Hey, you'd better not let anyone hear you say that.

MEGAN.  Say what? Fuck?

BILLY.  Don't! You'll get us in trouble.

MEGAN.  For what?

BILLY.  You can't talk that way. My parents spanked me once for cursing.

MEGAN.  They struck you? Have you spoken to a lawyer? I'm not an attorney yet, but I should be in about twenty years. I'd advise you to repress those memories until I've passed the bar. Then come look me up. *(She opens her lunch box and hands Billy a business card. He looks at it befuddled and then looks back at her.)*

BILLY.  What are you talking about?

MEGAN. You've got rights. No one can strike you for exercising your First Amendment right to the freedom of speech. Let me represent you. We'll take this all the way to the Supreme Court.

BILLY. *(Pause.)* I can count to one hundred and I know my ABC's.

MEGAN. I finished first in my class at Miss Hall's Country Day Kindergarten. My parents are sending copies of my report cards to Brearley, Trinity and Spence to see about early admission to high school. After prep school I shall probably attend Yale for my undergraduate work and Harvard for law school. Father thought I should go to Harvard undergrad too, but Mother convinced him going to both would give me twice the networking potential. *(Slight pause.)* So, where did you go to kindergarten?

BILLY. The West Side Eager Learning Center for Young People.

MEGAN. Never heard of it.

BILLY. It's just a few blocks from my house.

MEGAN. How did you get in here?

BILLY. My mommy brought me.

MEGAN. Ahh. Connections.

BILLY. How did you get here?

MEGAN. Rosa, my Guatemalan nanny, brought me. She's teaching me Spanish. Now when we go out to dinner I always ask for the check in Spanish. "La quenta, por favor."

BILLY. I hope we get hamburgers and French fries for lunch. Don't you?

MEGAN. Oh, no. I'm watching my weight.

BILLY. How much do you weigh?

MEGAN. Almost fifty pounds.

BILLY. I wonder if I'm in the right room.

MEGAN. When I'm no longer age-challenged I'm going to take on the really important cases. The big media circuses, with celebrity deaths and lurid details of sexual deviance. I'll drag the cases out with bogus appeals and grab all the headlines. Then when it's all over I'll sign a seven-figure book deal. Whether my client wins or loses. *(Slight pause.)* Don't you just love America?

BILLY. Uh … I like Hot Wheels.

MEGAN. *(Slight pause.)* What are those?

BILLY. Hot Wheels? They're toy cars. Mine go really fast.

MEGAN. My parents have a Saab 9000. It goes from zero to sixty in five seconds. What kind of car do your parents drive?

BILLY. We don't have a car.

MEGAN. What? How do you get to your country house?

BILLY. We've only got one house.

MEGAN. But where do you go in the summer?

BILLY. I go to the park or over to my friend's house.

MEGAN. You go to other people's homes?

BILLY. Yeah.

MEGAN. What do you do there?

BILLY. We play.

MEGAN. What do you mean, play?

BILLY. You know … games, pretend. *(Slight pause.)* Like my friends Brand and John and me play Batman. But none of us want to be Robin, and we all want to be Batman. So instead, one of us will be Batman, and one of us will be Bat*dog,* and the other is Bat*cat.* That way all of us can be Batman. *(Slight pause.)* Sort of.

MEGAN. Who's Batman?

BILLY. Where are you from?

MEGAN. East 65th Street.

BILLY. *(Knowingly.)* Oh. *(He reaches into his pocket.)* See, these are my Batman action figures. I've got Batman and Robin and the Joker and Mr. Freeze. Here … you can be Batman.

MEGAN. What does Batman do?

BILLY. He puts bad guys in jail.

MEGAN. Oh … so he's a lawyer.

BILLY. Yeah, except he wears a cape.

MEGAN. Cool, let's play!

BILLY. Great! *(They play. Fade to black.)*

## End of Play

11

# PROPERTY LIST

Lunch box with business card (MEGAN)
Batman action figures (BILLY)

# ON THE EDGE

ON THE EDGE was produced by the Vital Theater Company (Stephen Sunderlin, Artistic Director) in New York as part of Vital Signs VIII on October 30, 2003. It was directed by Tom Rowan, and the cast was as follows:

GENE .................................................................... Tom O'Hare
SAMMY ........................................................... Anastasia Barnes


The play was also staged as part of the American Globe Theater and Turnip Theater Company's Seventh Annual Fifteen Minute Play Festival in April 2002 in New York. The play was directed by Tony Pennino, and the cast was:

GENE ................................................................. Clayton Hodges
SAMMY .............................................................. Rachel Jackson


## CHARACTERS

GENE — 17, senior in high school, sensitive

SAMMY — 17, a female classmate of Gene's, seen it all


## PLACE

A ledge and window on the exterior
of a New York apartment building.


## TIME

Early fall.

# ON THE EDGE

*It is night, and Gene, a young man of seventeen, stands on a ledge on the outside of a building, ten stories up in the sky. He is plastered against the wall of the building, not moving a muscle. Every so often, he glances down to the street, and scans it, before looking up again. Several feet away from him there is a dimly lit, open window. From inside the apartment rock music and snatches of conversation can sometimes be heard. After a few moments, Sammy, a young woman of seventeen, appears in the window. She sticks an unlit cigarette in her mouth and pulls a match out of a matchbook. She strikes the match against the book a couple of times, but it doesn't light. She tosses the match out the window ... and notices Gene. Long pause. They look at one another.*

SAMMY. Hey.
GENE. Hey. *(Sammy glances down at the sidewalk as she tears another match out of the book and tries lighting it. Before it catches though, Gene speaks up.)* Ah ... would you mind waiting a couple minutes?
SAMMY. Huh?
GENE. Cigarette smoke really bothers me.
SAMMY. Oh. Sure. *(Gene looks down and scans the sidewalk again. Sammy follows his gaze and then looks back at him.)* So, what's up? You're missing the party.
GENE. I'm just hanging out.
SAMMY. That's cool. *(Slight pause.)* How's the view?
GENE. I can see my building from here.
SAMMY. *(Slight pause.)* I know you. You're in my physics class, right?
GENE. Yeah.
SAMMY. What's your name?
GENE. Gene.

SAMMY. Right. Right.

GENE. You're Samantha. Sammy.

SAMMY. Yeah. How'd you know?

GENE. … You're in my physics class.

SAMMY. Oh. Yeah. *(Pause.)* So, what're you doing?

GENE. What does it look like I'm doing?

SAMMY. It looks like a major bid for attention.

GENE. With *my* parents? I stopped trying.

SAMMY. *(Pause.)* So, what's the deal?

GENE. *(Shrugs.)* I decided life's just not worth it.

SAMMY. Bummer. *(Pause.)* So, what're you waiting for?

GENE. Amanda.

SAMMY. Amanda Harris? *(Gene nods. Sammy looks over her shoulder back into the apartment and then back at Gene.)* You want me to get her?

GENE. No, I'm waiting for her to leave.

SAMMY. But then you'll miss her.

GENE. Not by much.

SAMMY. Whoa. That's harsh.

GENE. Yeah, well … so's life.

SAMMY. So, what happened? She dump you?

GENE. We weren't dating.

SAMMY. So, she wouldn't go out with you?

GENE. … No. Not really.

SAMMY. *(Slight pause.)* Did you ask her out? *(Pause.)* Gene?

GENE. I don't wanna talk about it.

SAMMY. Hey, I just wanna be able to tell people why you did it. I mean, I'm sure to be interviewed by the news and the tabloids. After they hose you off the sidewalk.

GENE. They'll know.

SAMMY. Did you leave a note?

GENE. *(Slight pause.)* No.

SAMMY. Do you want some paper?

GENE. Would you go away?

SAMMY. If you don't leave a note, how's anyone going to know why you did it?

GENE. Because I'm gonna scream her name out as I fall, okay?!

SAMMY. *(Pause.)* What if you can't finish?

GENE. What?

SAMMY. I mean, do you have this timed out? How long will it take? Probably the sort of thing I could figure out if I paid attention during physics. But, I mean, what if you only get to say, "Aman — !" before you hit?

GENE. I'll finish.

SAMMY. There's a breeze. What if the wind takes the sound away?

GENE. I'll make sure they hear me.

SAMMY. I'm just trying to help.

GENE. I think I can handle it. *(Pause.)* You know, this isn't gonna be pretty. I'm gonna split open on the sidewalk when I hit. If I don't jump far enough, I might impale myself on that iron fencing. So, unless you wanna have nightmares about this for the rest of your life, you might wanna go.

SAMMY. No, I'm cool. *(Pause.)* I don't think Amanda knows you like her so much.

GENE. I don't like her. I love her.

SAMMY. Whatever. You should tell her.

GENE. *(Pause.)* I can't.

SAMMY. It's gotta be easier than this.

GENE. Yeah, but this makes more of a statement.

SAMMY. A statement about what?

GENE. It's just more dramatic, okay?!

SAMMY. Oh! I know where else I've seen you. You're in all the plays at school, right?

GENE. Yeah.

SAMMY. No wonder.

GENE. "No wonder" what?

SAMMY. You theater people are weird.

GENE. We are not!

SAMMY. Dude, you're on a ledge.

GENE. *(Pause.)* You don't understand.

SAMMY. Maybe not. *(Slight pause.)* Does your shrink understand?

GENE. I don't go to a shrink!

SAMMY. Something to think about. *(Slight pause.)* But, you know, Amanda's not so great. She's got a hot body, yeah, but she's kinda obvious. I mean, she's the sort of pretty you like to look at, but I can't imagine what I'd talk to her about.

GENE. No, she's really nice. She always smiles at me in the halls at school, and I run into her sometimes when I'm walking my dog, and we say hi, and then she talks to Molly, and pets her. She's not like you think. *(Slight pause.)* I love her voice. It's kind of rough, but sweet.

SAMMY. Yeah, she's got a kinda sexy voice. *(Pause.)* So, where do you live?

GENE. What?

SAMMY. I live near Amanda too. East 78th between Park and Lex. So where are you?

GENE. Why do you want to know?

SAMMY. Jeez, I'm just curious. I thought maybe we could share a cab across the park.

GENE. After I kill myself?!

SAMMY. Oh, yeah, right. I forgot.

GENE. Stick around. You'll see.

SAMMY. Uh-huh. *(Pause.)* Wait a minute. You said you could see your building. This is the West Side. You don't live near Amanda.

GENE. *(Slight pause.)* I didn't say I did. I said I saw her walking my dog.

SAMMY. Oh, man.

GENE. What?

SAMMY. Tell me you don't drag your dog across town, hoping you'll run into her.

GENE. No. We just go for long walks.

SAMMY. Oh, man. You're like a stalker.

GENE. I am not.

SAMMY. Oh, wow. Now that's an angle for the tabloids. Wait 'til I tell people.

GENE. No! Don't! *(Slight pause.)* Please.

SAMMY. Then come back inside and talk to her.

GENE. No. I can't.

SAMMY. Why not? I'll help you find her.

GENE. Because she's got her tongue halfway down Bobby Chamberlain's throat, okay?! *(Pause.)* I ran into her when I was walking Molly last weekend, and we talked and she said was coming to M.J.'s party tonight, and I said I was too, and she said, "Great. I'll see you there. We can hang out." I've been waiting all week for this party. I thought, "Perfect. We'll talk a little, then I'll ask her out." I've wanted to for months, but first she was dating Dean and then Chris, but ... Well, I got here right at eight. I was the first one here. And I waited near the door. And I waited, and waited. And I drank a lot while I was waiting ... and then she came in. And Bobby had his arm around her neck. *(Pause.)* So, then I had to go throw up for a while. And when I got back she was making out with him on the couch. So then I went to throw up a little more, and as I came out of the bathroom, I saw them duck into

18

M.J.'s mother's bedroom. *(Slight pause.)* All I wanted was to hold her hand and smell her hair … and now she's down the hall fucking him! *(Long pause.)*

SAMMY. Bobby's kinda cute, you know.

GENE. What?!

SAMMY. Well, he is.

GENE. He's an idiot. We've been going to school together for eight years and he still can't remember my name. He's always … I mean, it's like other people just don't … He's an asshole!

SAMMY. Hey, he's not my type, but a lot of girls go for him.

GENE. Oh, go away! Please?!

SAMMY. The thing is you shouldn't have waited to ask her.

GENE. Like I don't know that! Like that's not the reason I'm out here. I'm a loser. I'm weak! No one wants to be around me. I get it! I know, okay?! *(Slight pause.)* I can't take it any more, all right? I'm tired. I'm tired of trying to "just keep smiling," like my mother says. Or go, "Well, some people are late bloomers." *(Pause.)* I can't. *(Long pause.)*

SAMMY. Gene …

GENE. What?

SAMMY. I've got bad news.

GENE. You're fucked up, you know that!

SAMMY. Amanda's gone.

GENE. *(Slight pause.)* Bullshit. I'm not falling for that.

SAMMY. You must've missed her while we were talking. I bummed that cigarette from her as she and Bobby left.

GENE. No! You're lying! I've been watching. I couldn't have missed her.

SAMMY. Okay, fine. Keep waiting then. I'm going back inside.

GENE. No, wait!

SAMMY. What?

GENE. You're just gonna go in there and tell people or call the cops. Or you'll tell Amanda not to leave.

SAMMY. I'm telling you, Gene, she's already gone.

GENE. I was watching.

SAMMY. Fine, she's still here. Me, I need a drink.

GENE. If you go, I'll jump.

SAMMY. Yeah, so? I thought you were gonna jump anyway.

GENE. But I'll jump now. And it'll be your fault.

SAMMY. I can live with that. *(Sammy turns and disappears into the apartment.)*

19

GENE. Hey! Sammy? Sammy?! *(Slight pause.)* Bitch! *(Sammy suddenly reappears in the window.)*

SAMMY. Wha'd you call me?! *(Gene flinches and struggles to keep his balance.)*

GENE. Jesus Christ! Don't do that.

SAMMY. What did you call me?

GENE. Oh, give me a break.

SAMMY. No one calls me that!

GENE. Everyone calls you that.

SAMMY. What?

GENE. Everyone calls you a bitch. *(Slight pause.)* And after tonight I know why!

SAMMY. Knock it off, asshole!

GENE. Or what? *(Sammy climbs out onto the ledge and starts inching her way toward Gene.)* What the hell are you doing?!

SAMMY. I'm gonna make you shut up.

GENE. You stay away! You ... oh, I get it. This is like reverse psychology. You say you'll push me, so I say, "No, no, I want to live."

SAMMY. *(Grabbing Gene's arm.)* No, I'm just pushing you.

GENE. *(Grabbing hold of Sammy.)* I'll take you with me!

SAMMY. Like I care.

GENE. Okay, okay, I'm sorry. *(Sammy releases Gene.)*

SAMMY. Whatever. Forget it. *(Slight pause.)* Hey ... this is kinda cool out here. *(There is a pause as Gene gets his breath back.)*

GENE. Oh, man, I am so fucked up.

SAMMY. You just need to talk to a shrink or something.

GENE. I don't think I could.

SAMMY. It's not so hard.

GENE. *(Slight pause.)* You go to one?

SAMMY. Yeah.

GENE. How come?

SAMMY. My parents make me go.

GENE. You're kidding. Why?

SAMMY. They're worried I'm a lesbian.

GENE. Oh, that's fucked! Why do they think that?

SAMMY. 'Cause I'm a lesbian.

GENE. *(Pause.)* What?

SAMMY. I like girls.

GENE. Really?

SAMMY. Yeah.

GENE. Whoa. *(Slight pause.)* What's that like?

SAMMY. I don't know. Probably like you liking girls.

GENE. Does anyone else know?

SAMMY. No.

GENE. What does your shrink say?

SAMMY. Not much.

GENE. What do you say?

SAMMY. That I don't have a problem liking girls.

GENE. Is that true?

SAMMY. Yeah. I mean, sometimes … no, I don't have a problem with it. My folks are kinda messed up about the idea, though. They said they'd like disown me or not pay for college or something. It's a drag.

GENE. So, what are you going to do?

SAMMY. I don't know. Try to hold out until I get through school and college … then get away or something.

GENE. That sucks.

SAMMY. I guess. *(They are silent for a moment.)*

GENE. My parents are nuts, but … not like that.

SAMMY. Good.

GENE. You wanna go back in?

SAMMY. In a minute. It's kinda fun out here.

GENE. Yeah, it's a rush when the wind blows by.

SAMMY. Yeah?

GENE. Yeah. Wait … here it comes. *(They stand there feeling the breeze. The wind picks up a bit and they spread their arms flat against the wall for extra support. Their hands touch, and they laugh, surprised. They take each other's hand and wait for the next breeze. The lights fade to black.)*

## End of Play

# PROPERTY LIST

Cigarette, matches (SAMMY)

# SOUND EFFECTS

Rock music, conversation

# WHATEVER

WHATEVER was originally produced by the Metropolitan Playhouse (Alex Roe, Artistic Director) in New York as part of "What's Old is New" Festival on May 30, 2003. It was directed by Adam Melnick, and the cast was as follows:

JESSICA ................................................................... Jane Petrov
LIZ ..................................................................... Darcie Siciliano

The play was subsequently staged by Playwrights Actors Contemporary Theater (Jane Petrov, Artistic Director) in May 2004 in New York. It was directed by Tom Paitson Kelly, and the cast was as follows:

JESSICA ............................................................. Darcie Siciliano
LIZ ......................................................................... Jane Petrov

## CHARACTERS

JESSICA — 20s to early 30s

LIZ — 20s to early 30s

## PLACE

The living room of Jessica's apartment.

## TIME

The present.

# WHATEVER

*A half-darkened living room, with a couch and coffee table, television and DVD player, etc. Jessica creeps into the room, holding a tennis racket at the ready. Her eyes dart about the room, from one dark corner to another. She takes two or three very careful steps into the room. Liz steps into the room, holding a tennis racket carelessly at her side. She clearly doesn't think there's any danger in this room, and is a little exasperated with her friend.*

LIZ. So, where is he?

JESSICA. *(Whispering.)* Shh! He'll hear you.

LIZ. So?

JESSICA. He might be dangerous!

LIZ. Jessica … it's a pigeon!

JESSICA. You haven't seen him. He's got this wild look in his eyes.

LIZ. Well, I suppose technically a pigeon is a wild animal.

JESSICA. I'm telling you he's evil.

LIZ. Evil? *(Spotting an empty wine bottle.)* Have you been drinking?

JESSICA. No. Well … just a couple glasses of wine.

LIZ. And did you eat anything today?

JESSICA. No, I wasn't feeling well. But I took a couple Benadryl.

LIZ. Uh-huh. Did you see this demonic pigeon before or after mixing the drugs and alcohol?

JESSICA. I'm telling you there's a dangerous bird in this room.

LIZ. So where is he?

JESSICA. He must be hiding.

LIZ. How'd he get in?

JESSICA. I heard this tapping on the window. So I go to look, and when I open the window this freaky pigeon zooms in, flies around the room a couple times and lands on top of the television.

LIZ. Is this for real?

JESSICA. Yes! And so, I'm like, get out of here! And he says —

LIZ. Wait, wait, wait! *"He says?"*

JESSICA. Yeah.

LIZ. The *pigeon* says.

JESSICA. Yes, I know how it sounds.

LIZ. Oh, good. 'Cause it didn't sound like you did.

JESSICA. So I say, "Get out," and he says ... "Whatever."

LIZ. Excuse me?

JESSICA. Yeah, in this real Valley Girl accent. "Whatever."

LIZ. That's it. I'm turning on the lights. *(Liz turns on the light. The room is a mess. Jessica crouches, waiting for the pigeon's attack. Liz looks around for any sign of the bird.)* There's no pigeon in this room.

JESSICA. Maybe he went back out the window.

LIZ. It's closed. See? Jessica, honey, I think you imagined it. Did you really have just two glasses of wine with the Benadryl?

JESSICA. I think so. But that stuff makes me really thirsty.

LIZ. I think you need to get some sleep.

JESSICA. I can't sleep with this thing in my apartment.

LIZ. There's no bird here.

JESSICA. Are you sure? *(There is no sound, but Jessica suddenly reacts as if she hears something.)* Wait! Did you hear that?

LIZ. No, there was nothing. Come on, let me put you to bed.

JESSICA. No, I can't sleep. I'm too wired.

LIZ. Then why don't you read a book or watch some TV 'til you get tired?

JESSICA. Oh! I bought a new DVD this afternoon. You want to watch a movie with me?

LIZ. It's really late, Jessie, and I've got to go home and get some sleep. I think you'll be okay, won't you?

JESSICA. Oh no, stay! Please?!

LIZ. It's just ... oh, all right. But just for a while. What'd you get?

JESSICA. *Breakfast at Tiffany's!*

LIZ. Mmm. What else do you have?

JESSICA. Why?

LIZ. Because I've seen it.

JESSICA. So?

LIZ. So if I'm staying, I'd rather watch something I haven't seen before.

JESSICA. But I love *Breakfast at Tiffany's.*

LIZ. But I've seen it.

JESSICA. How many times?

LIZ. I don't know. Just the once, I guess.

JESSICA. How could you see it just once?

LIZ. I saw it once, and that was fine.

JESSICA. That's ridiculous. How could it be "fine" to see *Breakfast at Tiffany's* just once?

LIZ. Come on. It's a good movie, but it's not — [*The Bicycle Thief* or anything.]

JESSICA. *(Overlapping.)* It's a fantastic fucking movie!

LIZ. All right, whatever. We have a difference of opinion.

JESSICA. Name one movie that's better than *Breakfast at Tiffany's*. Name one.

LIZ. Are you kidding? I can name dozens. I can name other Audrey Hepburn movies that are better. I can name Katharine Hepburn movies that are better. The only thing I can't do is name a George Peppard movie that's better.

JESSICA. You cannot be serious. You have to see this movie again, because if you don't think it's the best movie EVER then … I don't know. I mean, did you sleep through it the first time? Or maybe you were really drunk and passed out. Or you were so wasted you threw up all over yourself and had to stagger to the bathroom to clean the vomit off your clothes, because otherwise I'm having a hard time with what I'm hearing.

LIZ. Yeah, I'm having a hard time with that too. I think you need something to eat. What do you have in the kitchen?

JESSICA. Or did someone break up with you during the movie? Is that what happened with you and Kurt? Were you watching this when he told you he'd been sleeping with that actress for the last six months you were together?

LIZ. What?! What actress?!

JESSICA. Oh, you know. The slutty one.

LIZ. Could you be a little more specific!

JESSICA. What's-her-name with the short blonde hair.

LIZ. Claire?! Oh, my God! He slept with Claire, and you didn't tell me?

JESSICA. It was so obvious. Everyone knew.

LIZ. Not me!

JESSICA. Well, whatever. It's old news.

LIZ. It's new news to me.

JESSICA. Then you need a good movie to help you get over it.

LIZ. I'm not watching *Breakfast at Tiffany's*!

JESSICA. *(Almost wailing.)* But it's sooooooo good! *(Hearing the phantom sound again.)* There! You must've heard that flapping!

LIZ. Jessica, there's no bird in here. I swear. Listen, we can watch the movie, but you've got to eat something first.

JESSICA. I don't think there's anything in the house.

LIZ. Let me go check the fridge. *(Liz hurries out of the room to the kitchen. Jessica looks around the room again, carefully peering behind furniture or whatever, tennis racket held high. She finds nothing. Liz returns with a slice of cold pizza.)* Here's some pizza.

JESSICA. It's cold.

LIZ. Cold pizza's great. You'll love it. Sit down, have a couple bites, okay? Oh! And you never told me about your date last week. Philip, right? How was it?

JESSICA. It was nice. He took me to dinner and a Broadway play.

LIZ. Are you gonna see him again?

JESSICA. He asked, but I said no.

LIZ. Why?

JESSICA. I don't feel like it. *(Reacting to phantom sounds again.)* Damn it! You must've heard that!

LIZ. *(Pause.)* David's not coming back.

JESSICA. He might.

LIZ. No, he's not.

JESSICA. Well, not tonight, no.

LIZ. No. Never. They never come back.

JESSICA. It's a fling. It'll run its course, and then it'll end.

LIZ. Has David said anything — ANYthing — that would make you believe that?

JESSICA. He said he still loved me. He said he still loved me, and he didn't know what to do.

LIZ. That was weeks ago.

JESSICA. He still said it.

LIZ. Yeah, but he also said he loved this other woman too, right?

JESSICA. And that he still loved me, and didn't know what to do.

LIZ. And ever since then it's been pretty clear that what he wants to do is fuck her. *(Slight pause.)* I'm sorry, Jessica. Please, don't cry. I'm sorry. I'm just trying … I mean, you never talk to him any more.

JESSICA. We leave each other messages all the time.

LIZ. He screens his calls and then leaves messages on your machine when he knows you're at work. When was the last time you actually spoke to him?

JESSICA. Today.

LIZ. T — ! Today?! You didn't tell me that.

JESSICA. I don't have to tell you everything.

28

LIZ. Who called who?

JESSICA. It wasn't on the phone. I saw him.

LIZ. Where?

JESSICA. On the street.

LIZ. Well, what did you say?

JESSICA. First I said, "I love you, David."

LIZ. Oh, Jessie … And what did he say to that?

JESSICA. Nothing.

LIZ. There! See? You say, "I love you," and he doesn't even respond?! It's over.

JESSICA. I'm not sure he heard me.

LIZ. What do you mean? Why not?

JESSICA. *(Slight pause.)* I was on the other side of the street.

LIZ. Oh, no, no, no. Where did you see him?

JESSICA. Downtown. On Lafayette.

LIZ. That's near where he lives. What were you doing down there?

JESSICA. I was on my lunch break.

LIZ. You work in Midtown.

JESSICA. I was shopping.

LIZ. On Lafayette?

JESSICA. There's stores.

LIZ. There's a Crunch and a Tower Records.

JESSICA. Which is where I bought *Breakfast at Tiffany's*.

LIZ. Were you following him?

JESSICA. *(Slight pause, unconvincingly.)* No.

LIZ. Jessica!

JESSICA. I love him!

LIZ. Oh, my God! You can't do that!

JESSICA. Sure I can. It's easy. I tell you, people pay no attention to their surroundings.

LIZ. How long did you follow him?

JESSICA. Just a little while.

LIZ. How long?

JESSICA. I don't know. A couple hours.

LIZ. What?!

JESSICA. Okay, six hours. But I ran some errands at the same time.

LIZ. Jessica! That's stalking! You can get in a lot of trouble for that.

JESSICA. I know, but I can't help it. I don't get to see him otherwise.

LIZ. No, you don't. Look, promise me, promise me, promise me you won't follow him again.

JESSICA. How about starting Sunday?

29

LIZ. No, today.

JESSICA. But I need to see him with her. I need to see how he looks at her. I need to know. *(Reacting again to phantom sounds.)* Can't you hear that goddamn bird?!

LIZ. Jessie ... come here. Sit down. You're just torturing yourself. What possible good can it do?

JESSICA. Maybe I'll see it's just a physical thing or maybe —

LIZ. Maybe you'll see two happy people holding hands and kissing on the street corner.

JESSICA. Maybe she'll get hit by a truck.

LIZ. Okay, that's it. I can't listen to any more of this, and I can't watch you do this to yourself. I have to go. You do whatever it is you think you have to do, but I promise you you'll be sorry.

JESSICA. You think I'm not sorry now?! I hate myself, but I can't stop. This isn't fair. I deserve better.

LIZ. Yeah, so? Most people deserve better than what they get. I know I do. *(Slight pause.)* I'm sick of hearing people say they deserve a better job, or a bigger house, or a hotter girlfriend, or whatever. That's life. There's gonna be things you just don't get. That's all there is to it. You have to forget about whatever it is you think you should have, and be thankful for whatever it is you do.

JESSICA. *(Long pause, then very softly.)* Okay.

LIZ. What?

JESSICA. I said, okay. I won't follow him any more. I won't call him. I won't even think about him.

LIZ. You can think about him. You can talk to him or even see him. But you've got to stop loving him.

JESSICA. Yeah. I know.

LIZ. Good. *(Pause.)* Good. So ... you want to watch your movie?

JESSICA. Sure. Do you? *(There is the sound of flapping wings. Liz jumps to her feet, startled. Jessica, however, does not hear the noise.)* Liz? Do you want to watch the movie?

LIZ. Ah ... yeah, sure. Whatever. *(Liz sits on the couch next to Jessica, who takes the DVD of* Breakfast at Tiffany's *out of the box. Liz takes hold of a tennis racket and nervously looks around for the pigeon. Lights fade to black.)*

### End of Play

# PROPERTY LIST

Tennis rackets (LIZ and JESSICA)
Slice of pizza (LIZ)
Breakfast at Tiffany's DVD (JESSICA)

# SOUND EFFECTS

Flapping wings

# DOUBLE WEDDING

DOUBLE WEDDING was originally produced under the title "June" at the Workshop at the Neighborhood Playhouse (Harold Baldridge, Artistic Director) in New York as part of *Months on End* on May 24, 1998. It was directed by Steven Ditmyer, and the cast was as follows:

DEBORAH ........................................................ Nancy Georgini
MIRROR DEBORAH .......................................... Nancy Keegan
SARAH ............................................................... Vivian Neuwirth
JOHN .......................................................... Harold G. Baldridge

## CHARACTERS

DEBORAH — late 20s, early 30s, a nervous bride

MIRROR DEBORAH — Deborah's reflection
(and alter ego) in the mirror

SARAH — Deborah's mother

JOHN — Deborah's father

## PLACE

A changing room in a wedding hall.

## TIME

June, of course.

# DOUBLE WEDDING

*A changing room before a wedding. The central feature of the room is a large full-length standing mirror. But the frame is open and has no mirror or glass in it. To one side there is a side table with a bouquet of flowers on top. The bride, Deborah, in a wedding dress, stands on one side of the mirror, examines "herself," Mirror Deborah, who stands on the opposite side of the open frame. As Deborah moves, Mirror Deborah follows suit, mirroring all of her movements. Deborah smoothes her dress and checks the result. Satisfied, she opens a lipstick that she holds and begins to apply it to her lips. Her hand begins to shake, however, and she smears some of the lipstick across her cheek. She stops and rubs away the errant traces. She lifts the lipstick to her mouth again, but her hand begins to shake worse than before. She grabs the trembling hand with her free one, trying to control the tremor, but to no avail. She lowers her hands slowly and takes a deep breath. Footsteps are heard approaching. At this point Mirror Deborah slowly begins to break away and move of her own accord. Deborah plasters a smile on her face as Tracy, her mother, enters. Mirror Deborah watches them through the mirror, growing increasingly agitated.*

TRACY. Deborah, I can't believe this moment's finally here. Oh, look at you. You look beautiful! Are you nervous? Don't be. Everything will be fine. The hall is all set. Wait 'til you see the flowers. That woman did a marvelous job. Now, don't be upset, but your grandmother knocked over the table with the presents on it, but I don't think too many of the gifts got broken. *(Slight pause.)* I'm kidding! Oh, you should've seen the look on your face. Oh, my. It's just a little joke to break the tension, sweetheart. Not that you should be tense. Phil is wonderful. We adore him. Oh, listen to me. I'm telling you not to be nervous, but I'm going on and on and on like a leaky faucet. Or an open faucet. Or an open fire hydrant. How are you, dear?

DEBORAH. I'm fine, Mom. I feel good. *(Mirror Deborah can't take this any more, and she explodes, shouting through the frame of the mirror. Tracy hears none of what she says. Deborah might react a little, but she's trying to stay calm, cool and collected.)*

MIRROR DEBORAH. GET ME OUT OF HERE! PHIL IS A IDIOT! I HATE HIM! I'M DYING HERE, CAN'T YOU SEE THAT?! IF YOU WERE ANY KIND OF A MOTHER YOU'D SAVE ME!

DEBORAH. I'm a little excited now that the day's finally here.

TRACY. I'm sure you are. I was talking to Phil's parents —

DEBORAH. Aren't they great?

MIRROR DEBORAH. Oh, please! They're such snobs. I don't think their spines bend unless they've been drinking. His father insists on a cocktail before dinner. "Just one," he chuckles. Four martinis later, this drunk at the table is telling bad jokes and blowing cigar smoke in my face.

TRACY. Phil's father is very funny.

DEBORAH. Yeah.

TRACY. And Kate, Phil's mother ... she's nice too.

MIRROR DEBORAH. She'd take an ice pick to my head if she thought she could get away with it. To her I'm this slut from the city who stole her son away from their nice little suburban world. Never mind he was already living here.

DEBORAH. Kate's really welcomed me into the family.

TRACY. Oh, I'm so glad. Those relationships aren't always easy. Your father's mother was a little cool to me at first. It's so much nicer when everyone gets along.

DEBORAH. They treat me like I've been part of their lives forever. It's been great. I'm really lucky to have had such a great family like ours growing up and to find another one now.

MIRROR DEBORAH. Are you catching the subtext here?!

TRACY. You are so beautiful in that dress.

DEBORAH. Thanks. It means so much to me that it was yours. It adds a lot to the ceremony for me. It's a special connection to you. *(Mirror Deborah reacts in horror, and vents her rage at her dress as she speaks, pulling off pieces of chiffon or buttons, tearing a seam or a sleeve.)*

MIRROR DEBORAH. Are you kidding?! It makes me look like a cow! How did I let you talk me into wearing this instead of that slinky Vera Wang I loved? What the hell was I thinking?! A huge bow on my butt? Why didn't I just paint a big target there? And who invented these sleeves? Leg O' Mutton? What kind of a style is that? "Oh, yes, please make my arms look like the hacked off legs of a sheep. Thank you!"

TRACY. I love you.

DEBORAH. I love you too.

MIRROR DEBORAH. Oh, I'm just gonna be sick! *(Tracy gives Deborah a hug and holds her tight for a long moment. They both get teary and laugh as they wipe their eyes.)*

TRACY. Well … I'll go downstairs now. Daddy will be up to get you in a moment.

DEBORAH. I'll be here. *(Tracy leaves.)* I think. *(Deborah takes a deep breath and tries to relax. Mirror Deborah leans forward through the mirror frame.)*

MIRROR DEBORAH. Okay, let's get the hell out of here! This is a huge mistake. Phil's no great catch. We can do better.

DEBORAH. Okay, be calm. Wedding day jitters. That's all this is.

MIRROR DEBORAH. Jitters?! No, jitters would be butterflies in my stomach. These are kangaroos!

DEBORAH. Stop it, Deborah! No, Phil's not perfect, but neither are we. Two years of therapy and we still haven't gotten over not getting Barbie's Dream House when we were six. Phil's good for me. Everyone says so.

MIRROR DEBORAH. Of course. No one's going to come out and say, "Dump the loser." All of our friends are as simpering and self-absorbed as we are.

DEBORAH. I am not simpering!

MIRROR DEBORAH. The point is that Phil —

DEBORAH. No! No, he … he's considerate and sweet. He's good-looking. He makes me laugh. He goes to romantic movies with me, but never makes me see those stupid action movies.

MIRROR DEBORAH. That's your criteria for a good marriage?! Movie compatibility?

DEBORAH. No … of course not, but …

MIRROR DEBORAH. What?

DEBORAH. That's all I can think of right now!

MIRROR DEBORAH. Doesn't that tell you something? *(There is a knock on the door and Deborah's father, Kevin, enters.)*

KEVIN. Hi, angel. How're you doing?

DEBORAH. Oh, hi, Daddy. I'm … I'm fine.

37

MIRROR DEBORAH.  Dad! You'll get me out of this. Don't let the smile fool you! I'm making a big mistake! Offer me a way out. Come on, say it. "Now, are you sure this is what you want? Because there's still time to stop if you're unsure. All we want is for you to be happy. Are you happy, Deborah?" SAY IT!

KEVIN.  Listen, Debbie, I probably don't have to say this, and we think the world of Phil, but … well, I want you to know that your mother and I love you. And we'll always love and support you. So, I just want to be sure this is what you want. Because if you're having any doubts … well, all we want is for you to be happy. Are you happy, Debbie?

MIRROR DEBORAH.  *(Triumphantly.)* Yes!

DEBORAH.  *(Reacting to Mirror Deborah.)* Yes!

MIRROR DEBORAH.  NO! No, no! I didn't mean it that way! *(Mirror Deborah reaches through the mirror, grabs Deborah by the throat and proceeds to wring her neck. Kevin does not see the struggle as Deborah breaks free.)*

KEVIN.  Thank God! Because we spent enough on this wedding to bankroll a small country. *(Deborah and Kevin share a laugh and a hug.)*

MIRROR DEBORAH.  Yeah, that's hilarious, Dad. Real funny. *(Tracy reenters, holding a boutonnière.)*

TRACY.  Sorry to interrupt. Kevin, you forgot your boutonnière.

KEVIN.  Oh, right … here, can you do it for me? So … are you ready? Everyone's seated and the DJ is ready to fire up the "Wedding March." *(Kevin turns to Tracy, who carefully affixes the flowers to his lapel.)*

MIRROR DEBORAH.  That's it! I'm getting out of here! *(Mirror Deborah takes hold of the sides of the mirror and steps through. But Deborah turns and slaps Mirror Deborah, who stumbles back to her side of the mirror. Deborah turns to her parents.)*

DEBORAH.  Would you give me just a moment alone?

TRACY.  Well, sure, honey.

KEVIN.  *(Chuckling.)* Not getting cold feet, are you Deborah?

TRACY.  Oh, of course she's not, Kevin. Really. What a thing to say to a bride.

KEVIN.  Oh, she knows I'm not serious.

TRACY.  Whenever you're ready. *(Tracy and Kevin leave. Deborah and Mirror Deborah stare at one another. Deborah smoothes her dress and checks her hair. Mirror Deborah folds her arms across her chest. Their eyes lock.)*

MIRROR DEBORAH.  I'm not doing it.

DEBORAH. Yes, we are.

MIRROR DEBORAH. You rushed us into this. We've only known this guy for a couple years. I never should've left you alone with him.

DEBORAH. You are such a naysayer. You never take a chance. I don't know why I've listened to your carping all my life, because frankly ... you're an idiot!

MIRROR DEBORAH. Hey, I haven't seen you skydiving recently!

DEBORAH. At least I want to. You're just scared. *(Pause.)* That's it, isn't it?

MIRROR DEBORAH. What's it?

DEBORAH. You're scared. You're scared of everything.

MIRROR DEBORAH. Please! Not jumping out of a plane at ten thousand feet has nothing to do with this.

DEBORAH. It has everything to do with Phil. You're frightened of anything risky.

MIRROR DEBORAH. That's ridiculous. I never heard anything so ... All I've ever done was to try and keep us from getting hurt. If I left things up to you, there's no telling what would happen. Give me one good reason — one! — why we should go through with this.

DEBORAH. I love him. And he loves me. *(Pause.)* Now, shut up and pull yourself together! *(Deborah again smoothes her dress and checks her hair. Mirror Deborah hesitates but then follows her motions. Deborah turns away and picks up her bouquet of flowers. Mirror Deborah stays, looking in the mirror, and trying to repair the damage done to her dress, pulling a torn sleeve back up on her shoulder or rearranging her hair. She checks her teeth in the mirror and uses a fingernail to pry out some piece of food. She composes herself as Deborah returns to the mirror for one last check. Satisfied, Deborah and Mirror Deborah turn and walk in opposite directions. But Deborah stops at the door, her hand frozen in mid-air before ireaches the doorknob. She turns and looks over her shoulder at the mirror where Mirror Deborah has also stopped and has also turned to look back. They stare at each other. The lights fade to black.)*

**End of Play**

# PROPERTY LIST

Lipstick (DEBORAH, MIRROR DEBORAH)
Boutonniere (TRACY)
Bouquet (DEBORAH, MIRROR DEBORAH)

# INFANT MORALITY

INFANT MORALITY was first produced by the Workshop at the Neighborhood Playhouse (Harold Baldridge, Artistic Director) in New York in November 1999. It was directed by James Alexander Bond, and the cast was as follows:

TRISH ..................................................... Darcie Siciliano
STEPHANIE HACKETT ...................................... Leah Herman
PHILIP HACKETT ...................................... Troy Myers
PAMELA WARDEN ............................... Mari Gorman

The play was subsequently staged by Playwrights Actors Contemporary Theater (Jane Petrov, Artistic Director) on May 19, 2005. It was directed by Greg Skura, and the cast was as follows:

TRISH ..................................................... Ashlie Atkinson
STEPHANIE HACKETT ...................................... Nicole Taylor
PHILIP HACKETT ............................................ Rowland Hunt
PAMELA WARDEN ............................... Jill Van Note

## CHARACTERS

TRISH — 20s/30s, a nurse

STEPHANIE — 30s, affluent and feels entitled

PHILIP — 30s, Stephanie's husband, the same

WARDEN — 30s/40s, efficient and direct

## PLACE

The front desk in the admitting room of a hospital.

## TIME

The present.

42

# INFANT MORALITY

*A hospital admitting room. A nurse, Trish, is behind the main counter doing paperwork. Stephanie enters. She carries a large shopping bag from an expensive store.*

STEPHANIE.  Excuse me.

TRISH.  Yes, can I help you?

STEPHANIE.  Yes, I have something I'd like to return.

TRISH.  To return?

STEPHANIE.  I got it here a few weeks ago, and ... well, it's not me. It's just not comfortable. *(Stephanie puts the shopping bag on the counter. Trish looks at it, confused.)*

TRISH.  Ma'am ... this is a hospital.

STEPHANIE.  Yes, I know. My name is Stephanie Hackett. I was in here about three weeks ago. That's when I got it.

TRISH.  *(She looks in the bag.)* Ma'am, it's just that ... oh my God! This is a baby!

STEPHANIE.  I'm sorry to be a bother, but I'm an investment banker, you see, and, well, I thought I could bring it to the office. You know, like in one of those cute little papoose things. But it just sat and whimpered in the corner while I was working, and I couldn't concentrate. And my husband travels a lot for business ... so, I'd like to return it and get a refund.

TRISH.  What are you talking about?

STEPHANIE.  Is your hearing all right? I want to return this baby.

TRISH.  You can't do that!

STEPHANIE.  What do you mean?

TRISH.  It's your baby!

STEPHANIE.  Yes, and I don't want it any more. I just finished explaining the situation.

TRISH.  But we can't take them back!

STEPHANIE.  Nonsense. Everyone has a return policy. So don't ... Oh! You probably need the receipt! Why didn't you just say so?

*(She digs in her purse.)* Of course you need that. Otherwise I could've gotten this anywhere. Sorry. Here it is.

TRISH. No, I don't need a receipt. You didn't pay for the baby.

STEPHANIE. We certainly did. And it was very expensive too. Now, my husband is double-parked outside, so I don't have a lot of time here.

TRISH. Is this some kind of joke?

STEPHANIE. Are you new on the job? It's a baby. *(Slight pause.)* Are you saying you're not going to take it back?

TRISH. Finally!

STEPHANIE. Well, this is ridiculous. I mean, if I'd known that, we'd've gone to another hospital. *(Slight pause.)* I want to speak to the manager.

TRISH. What?

STEPHANIE. You get the manager down here right now. I'm not going to stand for this. I want a full refund. And not credit. Cash. *(The sounds of a baby crying emanate from the bag. Stephanie hits the bag.)* Oh, shut up! See?! It was like this all the time!

TRISH. *(Slight pause.)* I'll call the hospital administrator. You can take this up with her.

STEPHANIE. Thank you. *(Trish picks up a telephone and dials. As she speaks on the phone, Philip enters. He frowns and crosses to Stephanie.)*

PHILIP. Honey, what's going on? The appointment's for 2:30.

STEPHANIE. She says they don't accept returns or give refunds.

PHILIP. What? You showed her the receipt, right?

STEPHANIE. Of course, I did. *(Trish hangs up and turns to the couple.)*

TRISH. The hospital administrator will be right down.

PHILIP. What kind of an operation are you running here?!

TRISH. Sir, please lower your voice. This is a hospital.

PHILIP. And a pretty damn poor one too!

TRISH. Sir, if you don't quiet down, I'll have to call security.

PHILIP. You go ahead and call. If they touch me, I'll sue this place so fast it'll make your head spin. *(The man pulls out a cellular phone, which he brandishes like a club.)*

TRISH. My head is already spinning.

STEPHANIE. Can you believe the way she talks? *(To the nurse.)* Are you familiar with the phrase, "the customer is always right?"

TRISH. Are you familiar with the phrase, "crazy as a loon?" *(The baby cries again. Stephanie throws her hands up. Philip comforts her.)*

44

STEPHANIE. Again with that noise.

PHILIP. Don't worry. We'll get this taken care of.

STEPHANIE. I told you a baby would be nothing but trouble.

PHILIP. I know. I'm sorry, Steph. I thought it would be different. This is all my fault.

STEPHANIE. Oh, no. It's not you. *(Indicating Trish.)* It's her I blame. I just want to put this behind us so we can go on with our lives.

PHILIP. *(To Trish.)* Look, the agreement my lawyer can't find a loophole in hasn't been written. So, why don't you just take it back and we'll forget your rudeness.

TRISH. In a second, I'm going to do something to you with that cell phone that'll make your wife's labor pains seem like stubbing a toe.

PHILIP. Okay ... okay. Let's start over. I may have overreacted. I'm sorry I raised my voice. *(He pauses and leans forward.)* Now ... why don't you just tell me what it'll take to make this problem go away. *(Slight pause.)* How does two hundred dollars sound?

TRISH. You must be joking.

PHILIP. Okay. You play hardball. I can respect that. All right, five hundred.

TRISH. Oh, that's it! I'm gonna — *(The hospital administrator, Warden, enters.)*

WARDEN. What's the problem, Trish?

TRISH. I am so glad you're here.

PHILIP. Your name is?

WARDEN. I'm Pamela Warden, the hospital administrator. And you are...?

PHILIP. Philip Hackett, and this is my wife, Stephanie.

STEPHANIE. We came to return something, and this woman has been exceedingly rude to us.

WARDEN. Wait ... "return"? Return what?

TRISH. Their baby! They got it here ... I mean, they had it here three weeks ago. Now they don't want it, and they want their money back!

WARDEN. A refund?

TRISH. Yes. And when I told them we wouldn't take it, he tried to bribe me.

STEPHANIE. That's a lie! She tried to extort money from us.

PHILIP. I don't understand why you people are having such a hard time with this.

WARDEN. You can't "return" a child.

STEPHANIE. Well, that simply wasn't made clear to us. And that being the case, I feel the hospital should do the right thing.

WARDEN. I think this is a matter for the police.

PHILIP. That's it! I'm going to sue this hospital for every penny it has. We paid good money, and when we were dissatisfied you had an obligation to make proper restitution, but instead we've been insulted and made to waste our time.

STEPHANIE. And our time is very important.

WARDEN. You don't intimidate me. I can have child welfare here in five minutes. And then I think we'll be seeing you on the six o'clock news! *(The couple heads down into one corner of the stage to speak with their lawyer.)*

PHILIP. *(He dials his phone.)* Yes, Ted Pendleton please. Philip Hackett calling. *(The couple huddles around the cellular phone, and the rest of the conversation cannot be heard. Warden and Trish remain by the counter as Warden flips through a phone book. The telephone on the counter rings, and Trish answers it.)*

TRISH. Front desk? Yes, she's right here. *(She hands Warden the phone.)* It's your secretary.

WARDEN. Yes, Jen? *(Slight pause.)* What? He didn't! Do the parents know? *(Slight pause.)* All right, don't say anything. I'll be right up.

TRISH. What's happening?

WARDEN. Dr. Henderson was delivering a baby, and there were … complications. I've asked the board not to let him … well, anyway it's dead. The baby's parents, the Kendalls, don't know yet. Henderson snuck the body out of the delivery room. I have to tell them. *(Slight pause.)* You'll have to deal with these two.

TRISH. Oh, of course. I'll finish calling — *(Trish picks up the phone to dial, but Warden breaks the connection.)*

WARDEN. Wait a second. *(On the other side of the stage, Philip switches off his phone.)*

PHILIP. He says we don't have a case.

STEPHANIE. What do you mean?

PHILIP. That's what he says. Unless we can prove the baby is defective, and that it's the hospital's fault.

STEPHANIE. Well, it cries and defecates all the time.

PHILIP. He said he thought that was normal.

STEPHANIE. What are we going to do now?

PHILIP. We could try and bluff them.

STEPHANIE. Bluff them? That's the best you've got?

PHILIP. Can you think of anything better?

STEPHANIE. Maybe we could give it to someone. Like as a

housewarming gift. Or for a birthday. *(The couple confers quietly as Trish and Warden resume talking.)*

WARDEN.  It's the perfect solution.

TRISH.  What?!

WARDEN.  Think of it as a total organ transplant. But without the surgery.

TRISH.  But the Kendalls should know their baby died.

WARDEN.  Our job is to alleviate pain and suffering. Are you asking me to inflict the worst kind of emotional pain on them? Have some decency.

TRISH.  But this is no better than what the Hacketts are trying to do.

WARDEN.  Trish, I have to weigh all the pros and cons here. Right now we're facing two potential lawsuits. I can stop both of them before they start.

TRISH.  Money? That's what you're worried about?

WARDEN.  Do you know what this could cost the hospital? Hm? Court costs, skyrocketing insurance premiums. Millions. And that means doctors taking pay cuts … nurses fired. Do you want to be responsible for that? Try to look at the big picture.

TRISH.  It's not right.

WARDEN.  Right, wrong … We're dealing with larger issues here. Shrinking profit margins, for one.

TRISH.  But the Kendalls lost their child. This baby's parents are right here.

WARDEN.  Do you know who the Kendalls are? They're very wealthy. This child could have the best nannies and be sent to the best boarding schools. It might even have a pony. But you want to take that all away.

TRISH.  Well, no … I … the Hacketts are terrible, yes, but the child should be —

WARDEN.  Put into foster care? Shuffled from one home to another, grasping for some sense of stability for the rest of its life?

TRISH.  No, it should be put up for adoption. It should be placed in a loving home, with a good couple who really want a child and will love her and always take care of her.

WARDEN.  Trish … no one has that. *(The Hacketts stride over to the counter. Warden, smiling, turns to face them.)*

PHILIP.  Our lawyer advised us to try and talk things over with you more, and see if we can't avoid a court battle.

WARDEN.  Oh, absolutely. In fact, I've been reviewing some of our by-laws and I've found there is a procedure for the return of infants who … haven't met the expected standards of the parents.

TRISH. You can't do this.

WARDEN. Trish, you've caused enough trouble. In fact, I think you should apologize to the Hacketts.

TRISH. Apologize!?

STEPHANIE. I don't know what terrible things have happened to you, but you don't help anything by going around with a chip on your shoulder. It's very unattractive.

PHILIP. Can we get this done?

WARDEN. Absolutely. I'll have you out of here in ten minutes.

STEPHANIE. You've been such a help.

WARDEN. Oh, please, I'm just doing my job. *(She indicates the hallway and the Hacketts exit.)*

WARDEN. Be in my office tomorrow at nine. It's time for your job performance review. *(Slight pause.)* I wonder if the morgue might not be a better assignment for you. *(Warden exits after the Hacketts. Trish is left alone. She turns and notices they have left the shopping bag with the baby. She rushes over and peeks inside.)*

TRISH. Hello there. They forgot all about you. Are you all right? *(She pulls a bundle out of the bag and cradles it.)* Oh, aren't you adorable. I'm sorry. I tried, but … Well, don't worry. I guess you'll be getting a new home. And a pony. *(Slight pause.)* What's your name? Did they give you one? I'm Trish. *(She smiles at the baby, and then looks down the hallway. She looks back at the baby.)* But you can call me Mommy. *(Trish hurries out of the hospital carrying the baby. Blackout.)*

## End of Play

# PROPERTY LIST

Shopping bag with baby (STEPHANIE)
Cell phone (PHIL)
Phone (TRISH)
Phone book (WARDEN)

# SOUND EFFECTS

Baby crying

# A MOTHER'S LOVE

A MOTHER'S LOVE was originally produced by the Workshop at the Neighborhood Playhouse (Harold Baldridge, Artistic Director) in New York on February 4, 2000. It was directed by Craig Pospisil, and the cast was as follows:

MELISSA ............................................................... Leah Herman

The play was subsequently staged by the Manhattan Drama Collective (Patricia Watt, Producer) in March 2002 in New York. It was directed by Craig Pospisil, and the cast was as follows:

MELISSA ............................................................... Brooke Fulton

## CHARACTERS

MELISSA — 30s/40s

## PLACE

Should be left vague. It will be revealed.

## TIME

The present.

# A MOTHER'S LOVE

*Melissa enters wearing a conservative suit. She smiles warmly at the audience.*

MELISSA. Our children need to be protected, don't they? And a parent has to do whatever they can to keep their child from harm. *(Slight pause.)* D-R-U-G-S are everywhere, and I — oh, I'm sorry. My little one is here, so I have to talk in code. Just let me know if I go too fast. Anyway, D-R-U-G-S are everywhere. You see reports all the time in the news. It's going on right inside our schools. *(Slight pause.)* And that's not all. Kids are going to school with G-U-N-S and K-N-I-V-E-S. I don't know about you, but that scares the H-E-double-L out of me. *(Pause.)* I want to keep Theresa safe. She's a little girl, just four years old. Innocent. Kids should be allowed to stay that way for as long as possible. They grow up too fast these days. *(Slight pause.)* Life is hard enough. I'm sure we can all agree with that. Childhood should be a time when you don't have all those worries. I want to make sure Theresa has that time. *(Pause.)* I love my husband. Even now, I still love Kevin. Now, he thought it was time to send Theresa to school, and I know he had his reasons. School can be a valuable experience. *(Slight pause.)* But times change. School isn't the same as it was when we were children. My first day of school I was so scared about being separated from my parents and about being surrounded by kids I didn't know. Imagine how much more frightening that would be today, knowing that many of your classmates were A-R-M-E-D? *(Slight pause.)* Now, look, I'm not saying anything would happen while she was in kindergarten … of course not. *(Slight pause.)* But after that who knows? *(Slight pause.)* Will Theresa make it to third grade before she starts doing D-R-U-G-S at recess? And after D-R-U-G-S, how long will it be before she's drawn into a world of S-E-X? And S-E-X and D-R-U-G-S lead right to P-R-O-S-T-I-T-U-T-I-O-N. *(Slight pause.)* Did I spell that right? Let's see P-R-O … Well,

I mean she could become a H-O-O-K-E-R. *(Pause.)* Not my little girl. *(Pause.)* I tried to convince Kevin we should keep Theresa at home and teach her ourselves. But he didn't understand, and we got into a big F-I-G-H-T. I tried to talk about it in a calm, reasonable way, but Kevin lost his T-E-M-P-E-R and Y-E L-L-E-D, and that made Theresa cry. I couldn't have let that happen. *(Slight pause.)* Ladies and gentlemen of the jury … yes, I K-I-L-L-E-D my husband. But what I did was a form of self-defense. I was protecting my daughter the way any of you would. Theresa's too young to see the world for what it is. She needs to be protected. And that is why I am innocent of M-U-R-D-E-R. *(Pause.)* Thank you. *(Melissa exits as the lights fade.)*

**End of Play**

# THE AMERICAN
# DREAM REVISITED

THE AMERICAN DREAM REVISITED was originally produced as part of the American Globe Theater and Turnip Theater's Eighth Annual Fifteen Minute Play Festival in New York in April 2002. It was directed by Carleigh Welsh, and the cast was as follows:

CHARTREUSE .......................................................... Sarah Kay
JIM ...................................................................... Jonathan Smit
DELLA ............................................................. Erica Silberman
GRANDPA ....................................................... Michael Locascio

## CHARACTERS

CHARTREUSE — 17, a punk or goth girl

JIM — her father

DELLA — her mother

GRANDPA — Jim's father

## PLACE

A desolate stretch of desert in the southwestern United States.

## TIME

Summer.

# THE AMERICAN DREAM REVISITED

*The hot sun beats down on the desert in the southwestern United States. A cow's skull, bleached white, lies on the ground. Perhaps music from some spaghetti western, like* The Good, the Bad and the Ugly, *plays as the family walks into view.* Chartreuse, a seventeen-year-old girl, is in the lead. She listens to music through a pair of headphones and an iPod. Her parents, Jim and Della, walk in together a few steps behind. They cross the stage and stop to admire the view. Grandpa struggles on, gasping for breath. Chartreuse takes off her headphones.*

GRANDPA. Slow ... slow down.

JIM. What's the matter, Dad?

GRANDPA. You're going too fast. I can't keep up.

DELLA. It's really too bad you're so old.

GRANDPA. You're telling me.

CHARTREUSE. How old are you, Grandpa?

DELLA. Chartreuse, that's not polite to ask.

CHARTREUSE. Fuck you.

JIM. Don't talk to your mother that way.

CHARTREUSE. Fuck you too.

DELLA. Can you believe this?! It's just terrible the way children behave today.

JIM. They have no respect for authority.

JIM and DELLA. But what can you do?

GRANDPA. Well, for starters you could've spanked her when she misbehaved as a child.

JIM. No one fucking asked you, Dad!

DELLA. Now, Jim, your father just doesn't understand modern

---

* See Special Note on Songs and Recordings on copyright page.

parenting. His generation did things differently — wrongly — but it wasn't entirely their fault because that's how they were raised. Thankfully, our generation could see all of our parents' many, many failings, and easily avoid them.

GRANDPA. Secondly, you could stop giving her every little thing she asks for.

CHARTREUSE. Why don't you shut up or take a nap or just die already.

DELLA. Don't be so sensitive, Chartreuse. Grandpa's generation struggled. He had nothing growing up, so he never learned the value of having absolutely everything given to you.

CHARTREUSE. Whatever.

GRANDPA. That kid's a spoiled brat.

CHARTREUSE. Bite me.

GRANDPA. And what kind of a name for a kid is "Chartreuse"? What, Kathy would've been too common?

DELLA. Listen, Grandpa, one more word out of you, and I'll shatter your calcium-deficient bones like Jim's sorry excuse for a career!

JIM. Della!

DELLA. I'm sorry. I didn't mean that.

JIM. It's not your fault. It's my father's fault. He shouldn't have been talking. *(To Grandpa.)* No one wants to hear what you think.

CHARTREUSE. I'm bored.

GRANDPA. Look, can we go back to the car? It's really hot out here. And did any of you bring any water? I'm parched. *(The other three look at him.)* What?

JIM. Well, Dad … you see, the thing is …

DELLA. We're leaving you here.

GRANDPA. What?

DELLA. It's just that you've gotten so old.

JIM. And hard of hearing.

CHARTREUSE. And you keep forgetting things we've just told you.

DELLA. But mainly it's because you're so old.

GRANDPA. What are you talking about? I'm in good health. I just had a check-up. My hearing is fine. You people have started mumbling and whispering all the time. And I wouldn't forget what you said if you weren't so boring or talked about anything besides yourselves. And as for old, well … people are living longer all the time.

JIM. And that's part of the problem.

GRANDPA. Why's that?

JIM. Because we need your money. I mean, it's just sitting in your savings account. It should be in tech stocks, mutual funds, something.

DELLA. And you don't use it for anything except living expenses. You don't travel. You don't buy gourmet food or fine wine. You don't shop for antiques.

GRANDPA. I've already got furniture.

CHARTREUSE. Yeah, and it's old and it smells.

GRANDPA. You don't need my money. You've both got good jobs.

DELLA. That's debatable.

JIM. Della!

DELLA. Sorry.

GRANDPA. You're well-paid. You've got plenty of money saved.

JIM. Yes, but like you said, "people are living longer." Our financial analyst told us we'd need a lot more money invested to keep living the way we do into our golden years.

GRANDPA. Or you could cut back on a few things.

JIM. *(Laughs.)* Oh, Dad … that's so quaint.

GRANDPA. It's not like you need four cars.

CHARTREUSE. Hello? It's not the eighteen hundreds any more, Grandpa. No one today has just one car any more than people have just one face lift.

GRANDPA. I was born in [insert year 70 years ago].

CHARTREUSE. You are so missing the point.

DELLA. Look, Jim and I each need a minivan.

GRANDPA. Why?

JIM. They're very practical.

GRANDPA. But why do each of you need one?

DELLA. So one of us can pick up the groceries, while the other takes the kids to soccer practice.

GRANDPA. You've only got one kid. And she never played soccer.

JIM. And we need a rugged sport utility vehicle for those rough and tumble weekends in the country.

GRANDPA. You use that thing to drive to work in the city. And as for that stupid sports car —

JIM. You shut the fuck up about my Porsche, old man! I need that car, do you hear me?! I'm forty-seven! I NEED that car!

DELLA. We're getting off the topic here.

JIM. Look, I'm sorry, Dad, but this is how it is. We love you. Really. We all do. Right? *(Della and Chartreuse shrug.)* See? We love you, and we're really going to miss you. *(Slight pause.)* But we don't need you. We need the money.

GRANDPA. So, what's your master plan here? Bash my head in with a rock?

JIM. No, Dad, of course not. I couldn't hurt you.

GRANDPA. Then what, you're going to love me to death out here?

DELLA. We're not going to kill you at all. We're just going to tie you up and let you expire peacefully. Of exposure. And dehydration.

GRANDPA. *(Slight pause.)* You people are nuts. We should've drowned every one of you at birth.

CHARTREUSE. Is this going to take much longer? I've got a date tonight.

DELLA. With who?

CHARTREUSE. The lead singer for Scuz.

JIM. Oh, no, no, no. I don't like the sound of that boy.

CHARTREUSE. Who says it's a boy?

JIM. What?! Are you saying that you embrace an alternative lifestyle?

CHARTREUSE. Maybe I'm just experimenting.

DELLA. Uh, excuse me, but can we get back to the matter at hand?

GRANDPA. No, no, go ahead. It's important that families talk.

DELLA. Oh, sure, now there's time to talk! Not that you could ever be bothered to talk to me when I needed it! No, every night you came home from work, and it was the same thing. A scotch on the rocks and a cigarette while you watched the evening news before Mom put dinner on the table. "Don't talk to me while I'm watching the news, honey." And at dinner it was, "Don't speak unless you're spoken to, Della." And if I had a question about my homework it was, "Ask your mother." No, the only time you wanted to talk to me was at bedtime, and then it was, "Let Daddy tuck you in, sweetheart. Oh, aren't you a pretty girl now. You're growing up so fast. Look at you. You won't tell your mother if I do this, will you? It'll be our little secret." So, don't you tell me it's important for families to talk … DAD! *(There is a long pause.)*

GRANDPA. I'm not your father.

DELLA. Oh. Well, whatever! You're all the same.

JIM. No, we were pretty close actually. Hey, Dad, remember playing badminton in the back yard?

CHARTREUSE. Can we tie him up and get out of here?

JIM. Oh, right. Best to keep this on a business level. You want to give me the rope, Della?

DELLA. *(Slight pause.)* You were supposed to bring it.

JIM. I thought you said you would.

DELLA. Goddamnit! Well, you'd better run back to the car.

60

JIM. Run? It's five miles. And it's really hot.

DELLA. Then I guess you should've remembered the rope!

CHARTREUSE. Oh for Christ's sake, here. Use my handcuffs. *(Chartreuse produces a pair of handcuffs. They all look at her.)*

DELLA. Why do you have those?

CHARTREUSE. Why do you think?

JIM. I've got a good mind to ground you, young lady!

CHARTREUSE. I'm already grounded.

DELLA. Then how can you have a date tonight?

CHARTREUSE. Because I don't listen to you.

JIM. Oh, give me those. *(Jim takes the cuffs and snaps one around his father's wrist. He looks around, but there is nothing to attach the other end to.)* What should I cuff him to?

GRANDPA. Criminal geniuses, that's what you are.

DELLA. Be quiet and let me think.

GRANDPA. Just out of curiosity, how is killing me supposed to help you financially?

CHARTREUSE. Uh, it's called a will.

GRANDPA. What makes you people think I left any of my money to the likes of you?

DELLA. What?

GRANDPA. How do you know I didn't leave every penny to different charities? Schools, Greenpeace ... theater companies.

JIM. Don't be ridiculous.

GRANDPA. Hey, I'm old, not stupid. Write a will leaving my estate to the three of you? Ha ha ha! *(Grandpa begins laughing hysterically, rolling on the ground, feet in the air, as the others watch him.)*

DELLA. *(To Jim.)* Would he?

JIM. No, of course not. *(Slight pause.)* I don't think.

CHARTREUSE. Hey, this is serious. I need that money. I've got my whole life ahead of me. I don't have the time to work. I need that money for all sorts of things right now. A car, the right clothes, drugs. Maybe even college.

DELLA. Why didn't you check his will?

JIM. I'm his only child. I thought he loved me. *(To Grandpa.)* Do you? Do you love me? Did you ever love me?!

GRANDPA. Oh, give it a rest. Listen here, you three keep me alive. Take real good care of me, and you can have all the money ... when I die a natural death.

JIM. Damn you! *(Jim attacks his father. They struggle. Jim chokes Grandpa, smashing his head against the ground. Della and Chartreuse run forward and pull Jim off his father, who lies very still on the ground.)*

CHARTREUSE. Oh man, he's not moving!

DELLA. If he was telling the truth about his will we've got to get him to a hospital before he dies.

JIM. Oh, he's faking.

DELLA. He's bleeding profusely.

JIM. But we'd have to carry him. And I'm tired.

CHARTREUSE. Let's get out of here.

DELLA. All right. We'll leave him here. Maybe he was lying about the will. If not, maybe we can forge his signature on his Social Security checks.

JIM. Okay. *(Jim gets up ... but he discovers that he is handcuffed to his father.)* What the...?

DELLA. Damn it!

CHARTREUSE. Dad, you're such a loser!

GRANDPA. *(Stirring and lifting his head.)* Gotcha. Wasn't lying. Get me to a hospital, or everything goes to charity.

DELLA. *(To Chartreuse.)* Where are the keys?!

CHARTREUSE. Uh ... I think they're on Scuz's tour bus.

JIM. Dad, how could you do this?

GRANDPA. Saw it in an old movie. Way before your time.

JIM. Damn it. *(Slight pause.)* Okay, help me carry him.

DELLA. Wait a minute ...

JIM. What?

DELLA. I'm not going spend however many years as his caretaker. We put a lot of thought and planning and effort into this. I had plans for that money. I can't walk away with nothing.

JIM. We won't. I'm sure he's bluffing. We'll check the will when we get home.

CHARTREUSE. And if he's not bluffing?

JIM. Shut up and help me carry him. *(Della pulls a gun out of her bag.)* What are you doing with a gun?

DELLA. I brought it in case you were too chicken to kill him.

JIM. Della, don't be an idiot. Now we can't kill him.

GRANDPA. God, you're stupid.

JIM. Huh?

DELLA. Jim, darling, I love you, but ... well, if we can't have his money then at least I'll have all of ours for myself.

JIM. You conniving bitch.

DELLA. *(Raising the gun.)* Flattery will get you nowhere. Goodbye, Jim.

62

JIM. Chartreuse, you want my Porsche? I'll tell you where I hide the keys. *(Chartreuse looks at her mother, and suddenly dives at her. Della swings around, but not in time. She and Chartreuse struggle over the gun. There is a shot. Mother and daughter look at each other.)*

DELLA. You little brat. *(Della falls dead to the ground. Chartreuse now holds the gun.)*

JIM. Good girl. Now, get me out of here. Let's see if you can shoot through the chain on these cuffs.

CHARTREUSE. *(Slight pause.)* You know, it looks like everything is mine now.

JIM. Chartreuse ... the keys to the Porsche are really well hidden. You'll never find them.

CHARTREUSE. So, I'll hotwire it. *(Chartreuse shoots her father, who staggers and falls. Then she goes to Grandpa, who holds onto life weakly.)* Sorry, Grandpa. It was all their idea.

GRANDPA. That's okay, honey. I was getting old anyway.

CHARTREUSE. Yeah. Look, it's getting dark, and I've got to go, but here's some water. *(She pulls some bottled water out of her bag and gives him a drink.)*

GRANDPA. Thank you.

CHARTREUSE. Um ... I'm a little turned around. Which way is the car?

GRANDPA. *(Pointing in the wrong direction.)* It's that way. Right down that path.

CHARTREUSE. Oh, yeah. Thanks, Grandpa. *(Chartreuse stands and takes the water bottle.)*

GRANDPA. Wait, can't you leave me the water?

CHARTREUSE. No. What if I get thirsty? It's a long walk. Bye. *(Chartreuse puts on her headphones and bops down the path. Grandpa watches her go with a smile spreading across his face.)*

GRANDPA. Bye-bye. *(Slight pause.)* Watch out for those rattlesnakes. *(There is the sound of a rattle as the lights fade to black.)*

## End of Play

# PROPERTY LIST

Headphones, Walkman (CHARTREUSE)
Handcuffs (CHARTREUSE)
Gun (DELLA)
Water bottle (CHARTREUSE)

# SOUND EFFECTS

Gunshots
Rattle of rattlesnake

# THE LAST DECEMBER

THE LAST DECEMBER, originally titled "December," was first produced by the Workshop at the Neighborhood Playhouse (Harold Baldridge, Artistic Director) in New York as part of *Months on End* on May 24, 1998. It was directed by Jim Brill, and the cast was as follows:

WOMAN ................................................................ Aerin Asher
MAN ............................................................. Michael Locascio

It was subsequently produced by Playwrights Actors Cotemporary Theatre (Jane Petrov, Artistic Director) in New York on November 20, 2004. It was directed by Francine L. Trevens and the cast was as follows:

WOMAN ........................................................... Patricia Guinan
MAN .............................................................. Marvin Starkman

## CHARACTERS

WOMAN — an elderly woman, sweet

MAN — her elderly husband, bitter

## PLACE

The living room of their home.

## TIME

A cold December night.

# THE LAST DECEMBER

*An elderly couple sits in a living room. Gusts of wind can be heard from outside. The woman reads a newspaper. The man, his once-large frame now thin, sits in a chair close to a television, watching a football game. The sound on the TV is turned up loud, but the man has a hand cupped behind one ear to hear better. A telephone and a thick ring binder sit on a nearby side table. The woman glances over at the man and then at her watch.*

WOMAN. It's about time to go. *(The man does not reply.)* Nick? Daddy?

MAN. What?!

WOMAN. It's just about time to go.

MAN. I know that! *(The man does not move, but continues to watch the television. The woman puts down the paper and gets up, fighting her stiff joints.)*

WOMAN. Do you want some coffee before you go? *(Pause.)* Nick? *(Annoyed, the man uses the TV's remote control to mute the sound.)*

MAN. What is it?!

WOMAN. I said, do you want some coffee before you go?

MAN. No.

WOMAN. How about some hot chocolate?

MAN. No. *(The man returns to watching the game, but does not turn the sound back up. The woman makes her way out of the room. After several moments the man stirs and checks watch. He looks around the room.)* Mother? Mother? *(The woman ducks her head back into the room.)*

WOMAN. Yeah?

MAN. Say, how about a little coffee before I have to go?

WOMAN. I'm making some.

MAN. Oh. Good. *(He turns back to the television. The telephone rings.*

*The man does not move. The woman crosses to it as it continues to ring.)*
WOMAN.  Hello? Well, hi. *(Slight pause.)* Yes, he's just watching the game. *(Slight pause.)* Say … Daddy?
MAN.  What?
WOMAN.  It's Mary.
MAN.  Oh. Well, say, "hi" to her.
WOMAN.  She wants to speak to you. *(The man gets up and walks stiffly over to the woman. He takes the phone and she heads back out.)*
MAN.  Hello? *(Slight pause.)* Hi. How are you? *(Slight pause.)* Oh, all right, I guess. My hip is giving me a lot of trouble, though. If I sit for too long it stiffens up on me so blame much I can hardly walk when I get up. *(Slight pause.)* How's the weather there? *(Slight pause.)* It's been real cold here. We went out for a short walk yesterday, and the wind was so cold it just about went right through you. *(Slight pause.)* Yeah, I've got to go out pretty soon. I'm just trying to watch the end of the football game. The Vikings and, ah … ah, New England. The Vikings are ahead. They've got a real good team this year. *(Slight pause.)* Yeah, okay. Thanks for calling. *(The man hangs up and returns to his chair. The woman reenters.)*
WOMAN.  Coffee will be ready soon.
MAN.  Say, is today Thursday?
WOMAN.  Yes, it is.
MAN.  What time is it?
WOMAN.  It's almost midnight.
MAN.  Oh. *(Pause.)* They've got some real good players on the Vikings this year.
WOMAN.  They sure do. Are they still ahead?
MAN.  Yeah. They're beating New England by twenty-one points.
WOMAN.  My goodness. That's a big lead.
MAN.  Yeah, you bet. *(The woman shivers a little and rubs her arms.)*
WOMAN.  Say, are you cold? I think it's kind of chilly in here.
MAN.  Hm? No, I guess I'm all right. You can turn the heat up if you want, though. That's fine.
WOMAN.  I think I will. I'm a little chilly.
MAN.  Sure, go ahead. You know, it gets so damn cold here in the winter.
WOMAN.  I know it. It's gotten hard to take any more.
MAN.  We should've moved, you know. We should've moved south years ago.
WOMAN.  That may be.

MAN. Hell, everybody else did.

WOMAN. I know. It just never seemed like the right time, though.

MAN. Uh-uh, no, it didn't. It never does. *(There is a long pause.)*

WOMAN. You should get dressed.

MAN. I'm too old for this.

WOMAN. I'll check on the coffee. *(The woman leaves. The man holds the remote control close to his face and adjusts his glasses, trying to see it better. He finds what he's looking for and presses the button to turn off the television. The man gets up, but he has a lot of trouble. His hip seizes up and he winces in pain. The woman returns, carrying a cup of coffee. She gives it to him.)* Here you go.

MAN. I'm just kind of sick of this.

WOMAN. I know you are.

MAN. There isn't much point nowadays. Nobody cares any more.

WOMAN. Oh, I don't know about that. But you can stop if you want to. Nobody said you had to do this forever.

MAN. I'll go tonight. But this is the last time. They're just gonna have to find someone else.

WOMAN. I think that's fine. *(The man exits. The woman crosses to the side table and opens the ring binder. The telephone rings. She answers it.)* Hello? *(Slight pause.)* Yes. Yes, I know it's time. He's getting changed. *(Slight pause.)* Uh-huh. All right. I'll let him know. *(Slight pause.)* And everything else is ready? Well, good. *(Slight pause.)* Oh, say, could you throw another blanket in? It's awful cold. *(Slight pause.)* All right. He'll be right down. *(The man enters, wearing an ill-fitting red Santa Claus suit. It is old and several sizes too big for him. He walks to the center of the room and looks down at the suit.)*

MAN. I'm not worth a damn any more. *(The woman carries the ring binder over to him.)*

WOMAN. Don't say that. Now, here's the list. *(The man holds the list up close and adjusts his glasses, trying to read it.)*

MAN. I can't read this thing.

WOMAN. Not at all?

MAN. No, I can hardly see it. *(Slight pause.)* I think you're gonna have to come and help me read this.

WOMAN. ... Go with you? Well, sure. Hold on. I'll get my coat. *(She hurries out of the room and returns a moment later, pulling on a winter coat. The man reaches into one of his large pockets and pulls out a small package, wrapped in bright shiny paper with curled ribbons.*

*He holds it out to the woman.)*
MAN.  This is for you.
WOMAN.  But it's early.
MAN.  No. You're just the first stop.
WOMAN.  Why, thank you.
MAN.  Aren't you going to open it?
WOMAN.  No. I think I'll wait until morning.
MAN.  All right. We'd better get going. *(The woman takes his hand.)*
WOMAN.  Merry Christmas.
MAN.  Merry Christmas. *(They smile at one another and leave. Sleigh bells can be heard as the lights fade out.)*

## End of Play

# PROPERTY LIST

Newspaper (WOMAN)
Remote control (MAN)
Coffee (WOMAN)
Ring binder (WOMAN)
Present (MAN)

# SOUND EFFECTS

Gusts of wind
Football game on TV
Phone rings
Sleigh bells

# NEW PLAYS

★ **INTIMATE APPAREL by Lynn Nottage.** The moving and lyrical story of a turn-of-the-century black seamstress whose gifted hands and sewing machine are the tools she uses to fashion her dreams from the whole cloth of her life's experiences. "…Nottage's play has a delicacy and eloquence that seem absolutely right for the time she is depicting…" *–NY Daily News.* "…thoughtful, affecting…The play offers poignant commentary on an era when the cut and color of one's dress—and of course, skin—determined whom one could and could not marry, sleep with, even talk to in public." *–Variety.* [2M, 4W] ISBN: 0-8222-2009-1

★ **BROOKLYN BOY by Donald Margulies.** A witty and insightful look at what happens to a writer when his novel hits the bestseller list. "The characters are beautifully drawn, the dialogue sparkles…" *–nytheatre.com.* "Few playwrights have the mastery to smartly investigate so much through a laugh-out-loud comedy that combines the vintage subject matter of successful writer-returning-to-ethnic-roots with the familiar mid-life crisis." *–Show Business Weekly.* [4M, 3W] ISBN: 0-8222-2074-1

★ **CROWNS by Regina Taylor.** Hats become a springboard for an exploration of black history and identity in this celebratory musical play. "Taylor pulls off a Hat Trick: She scores thrice, turning CROWNS into an artful amalgamation of oral history, fashion show, and musical theater…" *–TheatreMania.com.* "…wholly theatrical…Ms. Taylor has created a show that seems to arise out of spontaneous combustion, as if a bevy of department-store customers simultaneously decided to stage a revival meeting in the changing room." *–NY Times.* [1M, 6W (2 musicians)] ISBN: 0-8222-1963-8

★ **EXITS AND ENTRANCES by Athol Fugard.** The story of a relationship between a young playwright on the threshold of his career and an aging actor who has reached the end of his. "[Fugard] can say more with a single line than most playwrights convey in an entire script…Paraphrasing the title, it's safe to say this drama, making its memorable entrance into our consciousness, is unlikely to exit as long as a theater exists for exceptional work." *–Variety.* "A thought-provoking, elegant and engrossing new play…" *–Hollywood Reporter.* [2M] ISBN: 0-8222-2041-5

★ **BUG by Tracy Letts.** A thriller featuring a pair of star-crossed lovers in an Oklahoma City motel facing a bug invasion, paranoia, conspiracy theories and twisted psychological motives. "…obscenely exciting…top-flight craftsmanship. Buckle up and brace yourself…" *–NY Times.* "…[a] thoroughly outrageous and thoroughly entertaining play…the possibility of enemies, real and imagined, to squash has never been more theatrical." *–A.P.* [3M, 2W] ISBN: 0-8222-2016-4

★ **THOM PAIN (BASED ON NOTHING) by Will Eno.** An ordinary man muses on childhood, yearning, disappointment and loss, as he draws the audience into his last-ditch plea for empathy and enlightenment. "It's one of those treasured nights in the theater—treasured nights anywhere, for that matter—that can leave you both breathless with exhilaration and…in a puddle of tears." *–NY Times.* "Eno's words…are familiar, but proffered in a way that is constantly contradictory to our expectations. Beckett is certainly among his literary ancestors." *–nytheatre.com.* [1M] ISBN: 0-8222-2076-8

★ **THE LONG CHRISTMAS RIDE HOME by Paula Vogel.** Past, present and future collide on a snowy Christmas Eve for a troubled family of five. "…[a] lovely and hauntingly original family drama…a work that breathes so much life into the theater." *–Time Out.* "…[a] delicate visual feast…" *–NY Times.* "…brutal and lovely…the overall effect is magical." *–NY Newsday.* [3M, 3W] ISBN: 0-8222-2003-2

**DRAMATISTS PLAY SERVICE, INC.**
440 Park Avenue South, New York, NY 10016  212-683-8960  Fax 212-213-1539
postmaster@dramatists.com  www.dramatists.com